KIDS CAN COOK

VEGETARIAN

Button
Books

Illustrated by Esther Coombs

CONTENTS

Key

Look out for these symbols in the book. They tell you if a recipe is vegan or gluten-free.

 Vegan (meat, fish, dairy, and egg-free)

 Gluten-free

BEFORE YOU BEGIN

Get ready to have lots of fun in the kitchen, learning basic cooking skills and making delicious vegetarian things for you, your family and your friends to eat.

Before you start, read through the recipe first to make sure you've got all the ingredients and equipment you need, and you understand what you'll be doing. If you need to prepare any ingredients (such as peeling or slicing), do this before you start to cook. And never start cooking without the help of an adult!

Using an oven/microwave oven

If you need to move any of the oven shelves, do this before turning it on. Cook food on the middle shelf of the oven, unless the recipe says otherwise.

Don't open the oven door until the cooking time is up, unless you think something might be burning. Always wear oven mitts when taking anything out of a microwave or oven.

STAYING SAFE

* Make sure there's an adult there to help you.

* Always wash your hands before you start cooking, and when you've finished.

* If you're wearing rings, take them off.

* Tie long hair back and wear an apron.

* Be very careful when using a sharp knife or vegetable peeler.

* Never leave the kitchen when the stove is on.

* Use oven mitts when handling anything hot, and put hot dishes onto a trivet or heatproof mat.

* Turn pot handles to the side of the stove to keep them safely out of the way.

* Be very careful when boiling things.

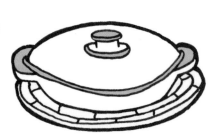

EQUIPMENT

You don't need loads of fancy equipment to make the recipes in this book, but here are some really useful things to have in your kitchen.

Spatula

Measuring pitcher

Food processor

Kitchen scales

Whisk

Oven mitts

Box grater

Large mixing bowl

Wooden spoon

Vegetable peeler

Garlic press

Potato masher

Baking sheet

Large metal spoon

Sharp knife

Cake pan

Cutting board

Citrus squeezer

BASIC TECHNIQUES

How to chop an onion

Put the onion on a cutting board and cut off the top. Use a sharp knife to cut in half through the root. Remove the papery skin.

Place one half of the onion flat side down and hold it firmly, with the root pointing toward your little finger. Cut across the onion to make slices and discard the end with the root.

To make the onion slices into dice, cut the other way across the onion.

How to chop an avocado

Put the avocado on a cutting board. Using a sharp knife, cut in half from top to bottom.

Lift the pit out with a large spoon and discard.

Run the spoon around the edge of the flesh and remove from the skin.

Place flat side down and cut into slices. Cut the other way to make the slices into dice.

How to seed a bell pepper

Cut the top off the bell pepper. You will see the core and seeds inside. Use a sharp knife to cut away the parts of the core attached to the bell pepper and pull away.

How to chop a butternut squash

Put the squash on a cutting board and use a sharp knife to cut off the top and bottom.

Run a vegetable peeler from top to bottom to remove the skin.

Stand the squash upright on the board and cut in half.

Use a large spoon to scoop out the seeds and any stringy bits.

Lay one half flat side down on the board and cut into slices. To make the slices into dice, cut the other way across the squash.

How to use a box grater

Place the grater on a cutting board and hold it firmly by the handle. Hold the vegetable (or cheese) in the other hand and rub up and down the grater. Be very careful that you don't catch your fingers or knuckles on the grater!

How to mince garlic

Cut the ends off a clove of garlic and peel it. Put it inside a garlic press and squeeze the handles together tightly. Use the back of a knife (not the blade) to scrape off any minced garlic that is still sticking to it.

How to crack an egg

Hold the egg in one hand, over a cup or bowl. Tap the middle of the egg with a knife to crack it.

Push your thumbs into the crack and pull apart. Let the insides fall into the cup.

It's best to crack eggs into a separate cup before adding to your mixture in case bits of shell fall in there too!

How to beat an egg

Put your bowl on top of a damp cloth to stop it moving around. Beat the egg with a fork or whisk until it's frothy.

How to sift flour

You need to sift flour to get rid of any large lumps. Put a strainer over a large bowl and spoon in the flour. Lift the strainer slightly and shake it from side to side. You may need to use a spoon to rub any large bits of flour through the strainer.

How to fold in

Use a large metal spoon to gently mix the ingredients. Move the spoon around the edge of the bowl, then fold the mixture over the center and cut down through the middle. Repeat until everything is well mixed.

DIPS

Serve these dips with crackers, tortilla chips, breadsticks, or toast. Or, cut a selection of your favorite vegetables into sticks-carrot, celery, bell pepper, and cucumber are all great for dipping. Each dip is enough for 4-6 people.

HUMMUS

Ingredients
1 x 14-ounce can chickpeas, drained and rinsed
1 small garlic clove, peeled
1 tablespoon tahini
juice of 1 lemon
1 tablespoon extra virgin olive oil
pinch of salt

1 Tip the drained and rinsed chickpeas into a food processor.

2 Add the garlic clove, tahini, half the lemon juice, oil, and salt. Blend until smooth.

3 If the hummus looks too thick, add a little more lemon juice and blend again.

4 Using a spatula, scrape into a bowl. Serve straight away, or cover and store in the refrigerator for up to 4 days.

GUACAMOLE

Ingredients

2 ripe large avocados, halved and pit removed

juice of 1 lime

pinch of salt

1/2 red chili, seeds removed and finely chopped

5 cherry tomatoes, quartered (optional)

handful of cilantro leaves, roughly chopped (optional)

1 Using a large spoon, scoop out the avocado flesh and put into a bowl. Mash with a fork until smooth.

2 Stir in the lime juice and salt.

3 Add the chili, tomatoes, and cilantro, if using. Gently stir to combine. Serve straight away, or cover and store in the refrigerator for up to 2 days.

TOMATO SALSA

Ingredients

4 ripe medium tomatoes, chopped

1/4 red onion, finely chopped

1/2 red chili, finely chopped

2 tablespoons extra virgin olive oil

1 tablespoon red wine vinegar

squeeze of lime juice

handful of mint leaves, finely chopped

handful of chives, finely chopped

pinch of salt

1 Put all the ingredients in a bowl and mix well. Serve straight away, or cover and store in the refrigerator for up to 5 days.

VEGETABLE CHIPS

Ingredients

1 parsnip
1 sweet potato
1 large beet
3 tablespoons sunflower oil
salt and pepper

SERVES 4

1 Heat the oven to 400°F. Using a vegetable peeler (or the slicer on a box grater), make long, thin slices of parsnip, sweet potato, and beet.

2 Pat the slices dry with paper towels, then place each vegetable into a separate bowl.

3 Drizzle 1 tablespoon oil into each bowl. Season with salt and pepper. Mix until well coated.

4 Put the slices on 3 separate baking sheets, making sure they don't overlap. Bake for 20–25 minutes until crisp.

5 Transfer to a wire rack to cool. Store in an airtight container.

Tips

* Beet juice stains, so it's a good idea to put on a pair of rubber or plastic gloves before you start.

* Some vegetables cook faster than others, so check each baking sheet individually to make sure they don't burn.

MUFFIN PIZZAS

Ingredients

4 English muffins, split in half
4 tablespoons tomato purée
1 ball of vegetarian mozzarella, grated
handful of basil leaves

MAKES 8

EXTRA TOPPING IDEAS
* corn * pineapple * olives
* finely sliced mushrooms, bell peppers, zucchini, or onions
* vegetarian Cheddar cheese

1 Put the muffins in the toaster. Lightly toast on both sides.

2 Heat the broiler. Place the muffins on a baking sheet.

3 Spread ½ tablespoon tomato purée onto each muffin. Sprinkle with grated mozzarella and top with a few basil leaves.

4 Cook for 2–3 minutes until the cheese has melted and is golden brown and bubbling.

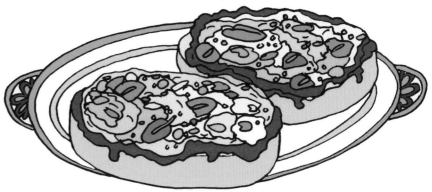

POTATO TOTS

Potato tots are made from grated potato and are shaped into little cylinders. They are crispy on the outside, soft on the inside, and very moreish!

Ingredients

4 tablespoons vegetable oil, plus extra for greasing

2 large floury potatoes, such as Russets, peeled and quartered

1 tablespoon chickpea flour (or other gluten-free flour), plus extra for dusting

salt and pepper

MAKES 20

1 Bring a large saucepan of salted water to the boil. Add the potatoes, bring back to the boil, and cook for 5 minutes. Drain and allow to cool.

2 Heat the oven to 400°F. Grease 2 baking sheets.

3 Once the potatoes are cool enough to handle, grate them into a bowl, using the large holes on a box grater. Stir in the flour. Season with salt and pepper.

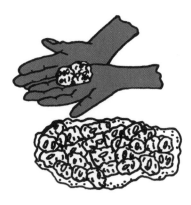

4 Dust your hands and the counter with flour. Shape the potato mixture into 20 small cylinders (short sausage shapes). Each potato tot should be about 2 inches long.

5 Heat 2 tablespoons of the oil in a large skillet over a medium heat. Add 10 tots to the skillet. Fry for 1–2 minutes on each side until golden brown all over. Remove from the skillet. Heat the rest of the oil, then fry the remaining tots in the same way.

6 Place the tots on the greased baking sheets. Bake for 10–15 minutes until soft in the middle and crisp on the outside. Transfer to a plate lined with paper towels to soak up any grease.

Tip

If you're not following a gluten-free diet, you can replace the chickpea flour with 1 tablespoon all-purpose flour.

SWEET POTATO RÖSTI

These Swiss potato cakes are delicious topped with sliced avocado and roasted cherry tomatoes. Rösti are traditionally eaten for breakfast, but they are the perfect side to any dish you enjoy eating with potatoes.

Ingredients

2 large sweet potatoes, peeled
2 tablespoons chickpea flour
  (or other gluten-free flour)
2 tablespoons vegetable oil
salt and pepper

SERVES 4

1 Lay a clean dish towel on the counter. Grate the potatoes onto the dish towel, using the largest holes on a box grater.

2 Pick up the corners of the dish towel and twist them together, squeezing the potato into a ball. Hold the dish towel over a bowl and squeeze out as much liquid as possible.

3 Tip the potato into a large clean bowl. Stir in the flour and season with salt and pepper.

  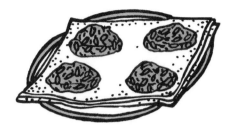

4 Heat the oil in a large skillet over a medium heat. Add the potato to the skillet in 4 piles, pressing each one down with the back of a spoon.

5 Fry for 5–10 minutes on each side, turning carefully with a spatula until they are crisp and golden on the outside and soft in the middle.

6 Transfer the rösti to a plate lined with paper towels to soak up any grease.

Tip

If you're not following a gluten-free diet, you can replace the chickpea flour with 2 tablespoons all-purpose flour.

Variations

Replace 1 sweet potato with 2 grated carrots or 2 grated parsnips, or one of each.

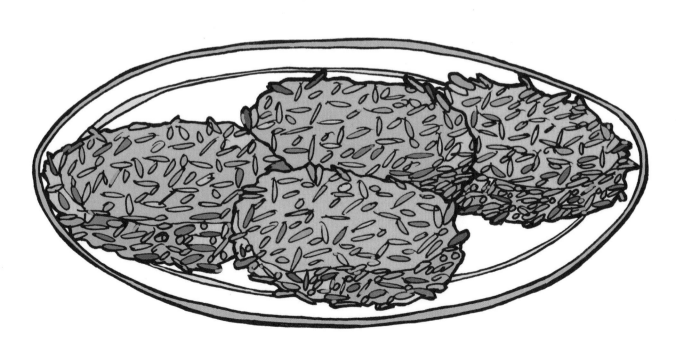

BAKED ZUCCHINI FRIES

Ingredients

½ cup all-purpose flour

2 eggs

1 cup panko breadcrumbs, crushed

2 medium zucchini, halved widthways and cut into sticks

salt and pepper

SERVES 4

Tip

To give the fries extra flavor, stir 4 tablespoons grated vegetarian Italian-style hard cheese into the breadcrumbs in Step 2.

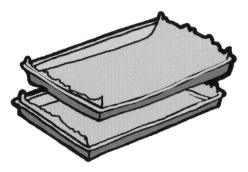

1 Heat the oven to 425°F. Line 2 baking sheets with parchment paper.

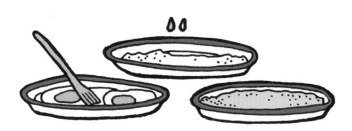

2 Put 3 wide, shallow bowls on the counter. Tip the flour into the first bowl and season with a little salt and pepper. Crack the eggs into the second bowl and beat together with a fork. Tip the breadcrumbs into the third bowl.

3 Take a zucchini stick and coat it in flour, shaking to remove any excess. Dip the stick into the beaten egg, then into the breadcrumbs, making sure it is evenly coated in crumbs.

4 Lay the breadcrumbed zucchini stick on a baking sheet Repeat with the rest of the zucchini sticks.

5 Bake for 10 minutes, then use a pair of tongs to turn the fries over. Return to the oven and bake for 10–15 minutes until the zucchini is tender and the coating is crisp and golden.

6 As soon as the fries are cooked, sprinkle with a little salt and serve.

BREAKFAST BURRITOS

Ingredients

1 tablespoon vegetable oil

1 red bell pepper, seeded and sliced

1 x 14-ounce can black beans, drained and rinsed

1 tablespoon butter

4 eggs, beaten

4 large flour tortillas, warmed

1 avocado, halved, pit removed, and sliced, or 1 x quantity Guacamole (see page 9)

1 cup grated vegetarian Cheddar cheese

salt and pepper

SERVES 4

Variation

Try replacing the egg with tofu. Put 14 ounces extra-firm tofu (drained) in a bowl and break into small chunks with a fork. Add to the hot skillet in Step 4, cook for 5 minutes, stirring occasionally, then stir in 2 teaspoons ground turmeric and a little salt. Cook for 3 minutes, stirring frequently, then remove from the heat.

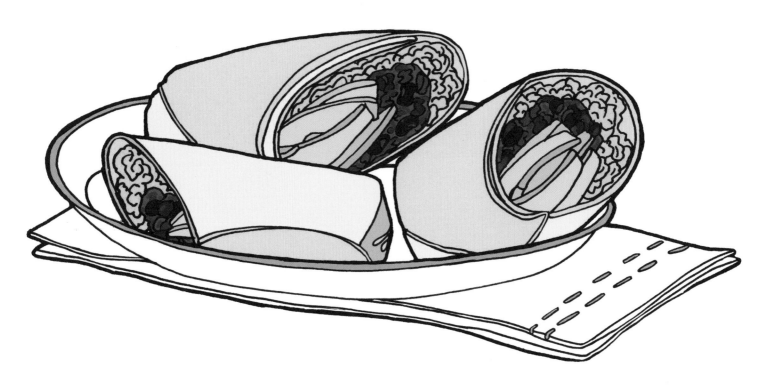

1 Heat the oil in a large skillet over a medium heat. Add the bell pepper and cook, stirring occasionally, for 5 minutes until starting to soften.

2 Move the bell pepper to one side of the skillet and tip in the beans. Cook for 2 minutes. Mash the beans lightly with a fork or potato masher, then tip the bells pepper and mashed beans into a bowl. Cover with aluminum foil or a plate and set aside.

3 Put the same skillet back on the heat and add the butter.

4 Season the beaten eggs with salt and pepper, then pour into the hot skillet. Cook for 2–3 minutes, or until just set, stirring occasionally with a wooden spoon and bringing the mixture in from the sides. Once cooked, remove from the heat.

5 Place a warmed tortilla on a board or plate. Add a spoonful or two of the pepper and bean mixture to the lower half of the tortilla. Top with scrambled egg and a few slices of avocado (or a spoonful of guacamole), then sprinkle with cheese.

6 Fold in the sides of the tortilla, then fold the bottom up and over the filling. Keep rolling the tortilla up until you get to the top edge. Repeat with the remaining tortillas and filling ingredients. Slice in half and serve.

TOMATO SOUP

Ingredients

2 tablespoons olive oil
1 onion, finely chopped
2 carrots, peeled and finely
  chopped
2 garlic cloves, minced
8 fresh tomatoes, chopped
1 x 14-ounce can chopped
  tomatoes

3 cups vegetable stock
handful of basil leaves
salt and pepper

TO SERVE

gluten-free bread
  or croutons

SERVES 4

1 Heat the oil in a large saucepan over a low heat. Fry the onion and carrot for 5–10 minutes until softened. Add the garlic and fry for 2 minutes.

2 Stir in the fresh tomatoes, canned tomatoes, and stock. Bring to the boil, then turn down the heat. Put a lid on and gently simmer for 20–25 minutes.

3 Remove from the heat and stir in half of the basil leaves. Using a stick blender, blend the soup until smooth. Season with a little salt and pepper.

4 Stir in the rest of the basil. Ladle into bowls and serve with sliced bread or croutons.

FALAFEL

Ingredients

1 x 14-ounce can chickpeas,
  drained and rinsed
1 garlic clove, minced
handful of flat-leaf parsley
1 teaspoon ground cumin

pinch of mild chilli powder
2 tablespoons all-purpose
  flour, plus extra for dusting
pinch of salt
2 tablespoons vegetable oil

MAKES 6-8

1 Tip the chickpeas, garlic, parsley, cumin, chilli powder, flour, and salt into a food processor. Blend until the mixture is almost smooth.

2 Dust your hands and the counter with a little flour. Shape the mixture into 6–8 evenly sized balls.

3 Heat the oil in a large skillet over a medium heat. Fry until golden brown on each side.

4 Transfer to a plate lined with paper towels.

5 Serve with pitta bread, salad, hummus (see page 8), and a squeeze of lemon juice.

ROASTED VEGETABLE BOWLS

These bowls are packed with goodness. Give this recipe a try and then experiment with any vegetables, grains, salad leaves, dressings, and toppings you like.

Ingredients

3 tablespoons olive oil
1 teaspoon cumin
1 teaspoon oregano
1 teaspoon garlic powder
1/2 butternut squash, peeled, seeded, and chopped into 1-inch cubes
1 red onion, peeled and cut into 8 wedges
2 1/2 cups water
2 1/4 cups quinoa, rinsed
large handful of baby spinach, washed
vegan feta cheese, crumbled (optional)

FOR THE DRESSING
1 tablespoon tahini
3 tablespoons dairy-free yoghurt
1/2 tablespoon maple syrup

TO SERVE
sesame, pumpkin, or sunflower seeds

SERVES 4

1 Heat the oven to 425°F. In a large bowl, mix together the oil, cumin, oregano, and garlic powder. Add the butternut squash and mix well.

2 Tip the butternut squash into a large roasting pan. Bake in the oven for 15 minutes.

3 Remove from the oven, add the onion wedges, and bake for 15 minutes, or until tender.

4 While the vegetables are roasting, cook the quinoa. Pour the water into a large saucepan and place over a high heat. Bring to the boil, then add the quinoa. Turn the heat to medium. Put the lid on. Cook for 15–20 minutes, or until the water has been absorbed and the quinoa is tender.

5 To make the dressing, put the tahini in a bowl. Add the yoghurt and syrup. Whisk until smooth.

6 Divide the ingredients between 4 bowls. Start with a large spoonful of quinoa, then put some squash next to it, then some onion, and finally a handful of spinach. Top with crumbled feta (if using), then drizzle with dressing and sprinkle with seeds.

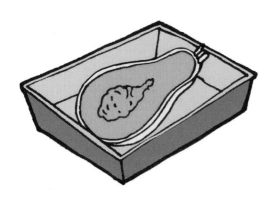

Tip

You can use the other half of the squash to make delicious cookies! Start by removing the seeds (you can leave the peel on) and placing it on a baking sheet. Heat the oven to 425°F. Bake for 1 hour, or until tender. Allow to cool completely. Now, turn to page 58 and follow the cookie recipe.

FRITTATA

Frittatas are super easy to make and a great dish to fill with all your favorite vegetables. Very similar to an omelette, they are quick to cook and delicious at any time of the day.

Ingredients

1 pound new potatoes, cut into 1/4-inch slices
1 tablespoon olive oil
bunch of scallions, trimmed and finely sliced
1 zucchini, sliced
7 large eggs
1 cup frozen peas, thawed
1/2 cup grated vegetarian Cheddar cheese
salt and pepper

SERVES 4-6

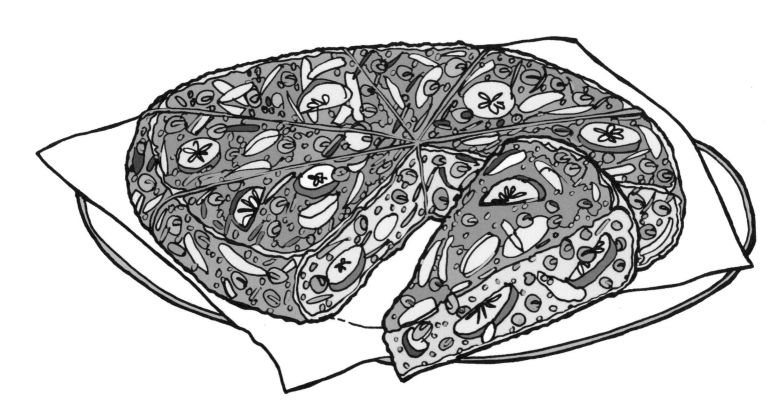

1 Bring a large saucepan of salted water to the boil. Drop in the potato and cook for 3–4 minutes until just tender. Drain.

2 Heat the oil in a large ovenproof skillet over a medium heat. Add the scallions. Fry for for a 2–3 minutes until soft.

3 Add the zucchini and potato to the skillet. Fry for 3–4 minutes on each side until starting to brown at the edges.

4 Crack the eggs into a pitcher. Beat lightly with a fork, then season with salt and pepper.

5 Pour the beaten egg into the skillet. Scatter over the peas and top with the grated cheese. Turn the heat down to low. Cook gently until the egg is almost set (it should still be a little runny on top). Heat the broiler.

6 Place the skillet under the preheated broiler for 4–5 minutes, or until the egg is set and the cheese has melted.

7 Cut into slices and serve.

EXTRA TOPPING IDEAS
* pesto (see page 43) * vegetarian goat's cheese
* vegetarian feta cheese * olives * chopped dill,
mint, parsley, or basil

RATATOUILLE

Serve **this** summer vegetable stew with fresh bread or pasta, or spooned over a baked potato.

Ingredients

2 tablespoons olive oil
1 large onion, finely chopped
2 garlic cloves, minced
2 zucchini, halved lengthways and thickly sliced
2 red bell peppers, seeded and diced
1 eggplant, cut into 1-inch chunks

2 x 14-ounce cans chopped tomatoes
1 tablespoon mixed dried herbs
salt and pepper

TO SERVE
handful of basil leaves, torn

SERVES 4-6

1 Heat the oil in a large skillet over a low heat. Add the onion and garlic and cook for 5–10 minutes, or until soft.

2 Stir in the zucchini, bell pepper, and aubergine. Cook for 5 minutes, stirring occasionally.

3 Add the tomatoes and dried herbs. Put a lid on the skillet and cook for 20–25 minutes, or until the vegetables are tender. Remove the lid and cook for 5 minutes to thicken the sauce.

4 Season with salt and pepper, sprinkle with basil, and serve.

HALLOUMI BURGERS

Ingredients
1 tablespoon olive oil
1 x 8-ounce block of vegetarian halloumi
   cheese, cut into 8 thick slices

TO SERVE
4 burger buns, spilt in half
1 baby gem lettuce, leaves separated
2 tomatoes, sliced
1 x quantity Hummus (see page 8)

SERVES 4

1 Heat the oil in a large skillet over a medium heat. Fry the halloumi for 2–3 minutes on each side, or until the slices are crisp and golden.

2 Transfer the halloumi to a plate lined with paper towels to soak up any grease.

3 To assemble the burgers, spread some hummus on the bottom half of the bun. Add 2 slices of halloumi, a couple of tomato slices, and a few lettuce leaves. Sandwich with the top half of the bun and serve.

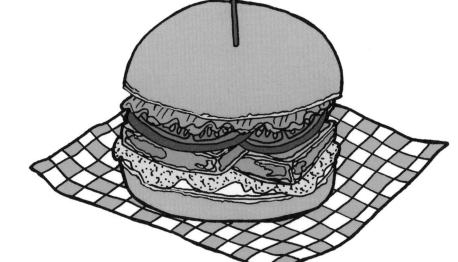

Tip
Toast the burger buns under the broiler before filling, if you like.

BEAN BURGERS

Ingredients

1 x 14-ounce can mixed beans,
    drained and rinsed
2 tablespoons vegetable oil
pinch of mild chili powder,
    ground cumin, or paprika
1 large carrot, grated
1 red onion, finely chopped
2 garlic cloves, minced
small handful of cilantro
    leaves, roughly chopped
2 teaspoons all-purpose flour,
    plus extra for dusting

TO SERVE
6 burger buns, split in half
lettuce
tomato ketchup

SERVES 6

1 Tip the beans into a saucepan and cover with cold water. Bring to the boil, then turn down the heat. Simmer for 10 minutes, then drain.

2 Put the beans into a large bowl. Mash with a potato masher or fork until almost smooth. Set aside.

3 Heat 1 tablespoon of the oil in a large skillet over a low heat. Stir in your chosen spice. Fry for 1 minute, stirring continuously.

4 Add the carrot, onion, and garlic to the skillet. Cook gently for 10 minutes until soft.

5 Add the carrot and onion mixture to the mashed beans. Put the skillet to one side (you'll use it again later). Stir in the flour and cilantro. Leave to cool.

6 Once the mixture is cool enough to handle, dust your hands and the counter with flour. Shape the mixture into 6 evenly sized balls.

7 Wipe out the inside of the skillet with a paper towel. Add 1 tablespoon of oil and place over a medium heat.

8 Add the balls to the skillet (you might need to cook them in two batches). Flatten with a spatula to make them burger shaped. Fry for 5–7 minutes on each side until golden brown.

9 Put each burger in a bun. Top with lettuce and tomato ketchup.

CARROT HOT DOGS

Ingredients

1 tablespoon maple syrup
½ tablespoon olive oil
1 teaspoon cider vinegar
1 teaspoon smoked paprika
pinch of salt
4 small carrots, peeled
4 hot dog rolls

SERVES 4

TO SERVE
tomato ketchup
yellow mustard
crispy kale (see
    opposite page)

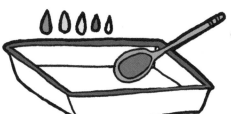

1 Heat the oven to 400°F. Mix the syrup, oil, vinegar, paprika, and salt in a baking dish.

2 Add the carrots to the dish and toss until evenly coated. Bake in the oven for 30–35 minutes, or until tender.

3 Open out the hot dog rolls and place on a baking sheet. Bake in the oven for 3–5 minutes, or until lightly toasted.

4 Put a carrot into each toasted roll. Top with ketchup, mustard, and a sprinkling of crispy kale.

Variation

Give these hot dogs a Mexican twist by topping with crushed tortilla chips, salsa, vegan sour cream, and grated vegan Cheddar cheese.

How to make crispy kale

Heat the oven to 300°F. Line a baking sheet with parchment paper. Wash 1 cup chopped kale. Dry thoroughly with a clean dish towel. Put in a large bowl. Add ½ tablespoon olive oil and season with salt and pepper. Toss until evenly coated. Tip onto the baking sheet and spread out in a single layer. Bake for 20 minutes, or until crisp but still green.

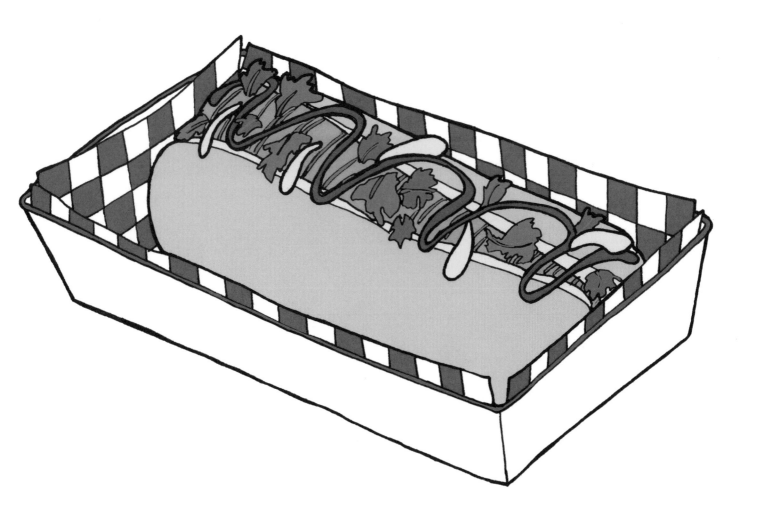

VEGGIE NUGGETS

Ingredients

2 tablespoons vegetable oil,
    plus extra for greasing
1 onion, finely chopped
2 potatoes, peeled
1 garlic clove, minced
1 carrot, grated
1 parsnip, grated
1½ cups frozen peas, thawed
1 x 8-ounce can corn, drained
½ cup all-purpose flour, plus
    extra for dusting
salt and pepper

SERVES 4

FOR THE COATING
2 eggs, beaten
½ cup all-purpose flour,
    plus extra for dusting
4 cups cornflakes, lightly
    crushed

Variation

For a cheesy center, roll the mixture into balls in Step 6, then take
one and flatten it out in the palm of your hand. Put a small cube of
vegetarian mozzarella cheese in the center, then fold over the edges
of the mixture to cover. Flatten a little to create a nugget shape,
making sure the cheese doesn't poke through. Repeat with the rest
of the mixture, then continue from Step 7.

1 Heat the oil in large skillet over a low heat. Add the onion and fry for 5–10 minutes, or until softened, stirring occasionally with a wooden spoon.

2 Using the largest holes on a box grater, grate the potatoes onto a clean dish towel. Pick up the corners and twist together. Hold over a bowl, squeezing out as much liquid as possible.

3 Add the garlic to the skillet and fry for 1 minute, then tip in the potato, carrot, and parsnip. Cook for 10 minutes, or until softened, stirring occasionally.

4 Tip the vegetables into a large bowl. Stir in the peas, sweetcorn, and flour until well mixed. Allow to cool, then cover and put in the refrigerator for 30 minutes.

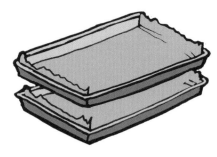

5 Heat the oven to 425°F. Line 2 large baking sheets with parchment paper.

6 Remove the mixture from the refrigerator. Season with a little salt and pepper. Dust your hands and the counter with flour. Roll the mixture into 20 evenly sized balls, then flatten a little to create a nugget shape.

7 To coat the nuggets, put the eggs, flour, and cornflakes into 3 wide, shallow bowls. Season the flour with salt and pepper.

8 Dip each nugget into the flour, shaking off any excess, then into the egg, and then into the cornflakes. Put on a lined sheet.

9 Bake for 10 minutes. Remove from the oven and turn over with tongs. Bake for 10 minutes, or until crisp and brown.

SPINACH LASAGNA

Ingredients

2 pounds spinach, washed
1 cup ricotta cheese
about ¾ pound dried lasagna noodles
¼ cup grated vegetarian Italian-style
   hard cheese
salt and pepper

FOR THE WHITE SAUCE
¼ cup (½ stick) butter
⅓ cup all-purpose flour
3 cups milk
1 teaspoon Dijon mustard (optional)

SERVES 6

1 Put the spinach into a strainer or colander and place over a large bowl. Pour hot water from the kettle over the spinach to wilt (you might need to do this in batches). Leave to cool.

2 While the spinach is cooling, make the white sauce. Melt the butter in a saucepan over a medium heat. Stir in the flour with a whisk or wooden spoon. Keep stirring for 1 minute, then remove from the heat.

3 Stir in the milk a little at a time, allowing the sauce to become thick and smooth before adding more milk. Once all the milk has been added, place the saucepan over a medium heat, stirring continuously. As soon as the sauce comes to the boil, remove from the heat. Stir in the mustard (if using) and season with salt and pepper. Set aside.

4 Once the spinach is cool enough to handle, take small handfuls and squeeze out as much liquid as possible. Place on a cutting board and finely chop with a sharp knife.

5 Put the ricotta in a large bowl. Beat with a wooden spoon until smooth. Stir in the chopped spinach and 1 tablespoon of the white sauce. Mix well. Season with a little salt and pepper.

6 Heat the oven to 425°F. Spread a little of the spinach mixture over the base of a large, deep baking dish. Cover with a layer of noodles. Spoon over some white sauce and sprinkle with grated cheese. Continue layering in the same way, finishing with a layer of noodles and the rest of the white sauce and grated cheese. Bake for 30 minutes, or until the top is golden brown and the noodles are soft.

Tip

If you like your lasagna extra cheesy, sprinkle over ³/₄ cup grated vegetarian mozzarella or Cheddar cheese before baking.

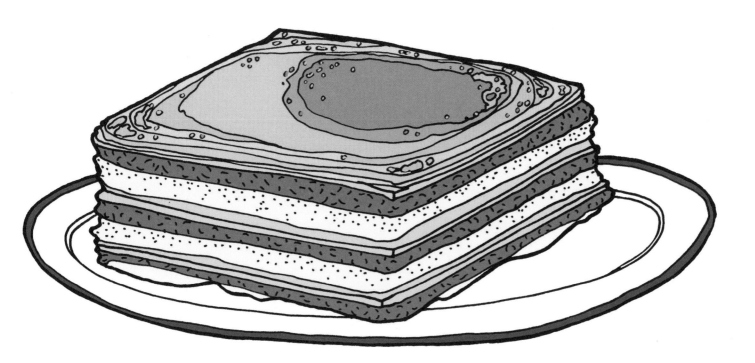

MAC & CHEESE

Ingredients

3 cups dried macaroni

1/4 cup (1/2 stick) butter

1/3 cup all-purpose flour

3 cups milk

3/4 cup grated vegetarian
Cheddar cheese, plus extra
for sprinkling

1 teaspoon Dijon mustard
(optional)

your chosen vegetable
(see below)

salt and pepper

SERVES 4-6

VEGETABLE IDEAS

PEAS

Add 1 cup frozen peas to the
saucepan 1 minute before the
end of the cooking time in Step 1.

BROCCOLI

Add 1/2 pound broccoli (or
cauliflower) florets to the
saucepan 5 minutes before the
end of the cooking time in Step 1.

KALE

Add 3 cups chopped kale to the
saucepan 5 minutes before the
end of the cooking time in Step 1.

1 Heat the oven to 425°F. Bring a large saucepan of salted water to the boil. Add the pasta and cook according to the packet instructions, adding your chosen vegetable before the end of the cooking time (see opposite page). Drain, then return to the pan.

2 To make the cheese sauce, melt the butter in a saucepan over a low heat. Stir in the flour with a wooden spoon or whisk. Cook for 1–2 minutes, stirring all the time. Remove from the heat.

3 Stir in the milk, a little at a time, allowing the sauce to become thick and smooth before adding more milk. Return to the heat and bring to the boil, stirring continuously. Remove from the heat.

4 Stir in the cheese, a little salt and pepper, and mustard (if using).

5 Stir the cheese sauce into the cooked pasta and vegetables and mix well.

6 Spoon into a large, deep baking dish and sprinkle with cheese. Bake for 8–10 minutes until golden brown and bubbling.

SPAGHETTI & VEGGIE BALLS

Ingredients

1 large carrot, peeled and roughly chopped
1 red bell pepper, seeded and roughly chopped
1 small red onion, quartered
2 garlic cloves, peeled
1 x 14-ounce can kidney beans, drained
   and rinsed
1/2 cup breadcrumbs
1/2 cup corn
3 tablespoons all-purpose flour, plus extra
   for dusting
2 tablespoons olive oil
3/4 pound dried spaghetti
salt and pepper

SERVES 4

FOR THE TOMATO SAUCE
1 tablespoon olive oil
1 garlic clove, minced
1 x 14-ounce can chopped tomatoes
handful of basil leaves, plus extra
   to serve

TO SERVE
nutritional yeast (optional)

1 Put the carrot, pepper, onion, garlic, and kidney beans in a food processor. Blend until very finely chopped.

2 Tip the vegetables into a large bowl. Stir in the breadcrumbs, corn, and flour with a wooden spoon until well mixed. Season with salt and pepper.

3 Dust your hands and the counter with flour. Roll the mixture into 20 evenly sized balls.

4 Heat the oil in a large skillet over a medium heat. Fry the veggie balls for 15–20 minutes, turning occasionally, until cooked through and golden brown all over (you might need to do this in batches). Transfer to a plate lined with paper towels to soak up any grease.

5 To make the tomato sauce, add the oil to the same skillet and place over a low heat. Add the garlic and fry for 2 minutes.

6 Tip in the chopped tomatoes. Half-fill the can with water and add to the skillet. Stir in the basil leaves. Bring to the boil, then turn down the heat so that the sauce is bubbling gently. Cook for 20 minutes, stirring occasionally, until you have a thick sauce.

7 Turn the heat to low. Season with a little salt and pepper. Drop in the veggie balls so they can heat through while you cook the pasta.

8 Cook the spaghetti in a large saucepan of salted boiling water, according to the packet instructions. Drain. Divide between 4 plates. Top with the veggie balls and a few basil leaves, and a sprinkling of nutritional yeast, if you like.

CAULIFLOWER CRUST PIZZA

Ingredients

2 cauliflowers, cut into florets
2 eggs
1 cup finely grated vegetarian
  Cheddar cheese
1 teaspoon salt
pepper

FOR THE TOPPING

4 tablespoons tomato paste
1 ball of mozzarella, sliced
½ red bell pepper, finely sliced
6 button mushrooms, finely sliced
handful of pitted olives, sliced
1 teaspoon dried oregano

MAKES 2 MEDIUM PIZZAS

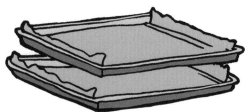

1 Heat the oven to 350°F. Line 2 large baking sheets with parchment paper.

2 Put the cauliflower in a food processor and blend until very finely chopped (you might need to do this in batches).

3 Tip the cauliflower into a large dry skillet and place over a low heat. Cook for 10–15 minutes, stirring occasionally, until the moisture has evaporated and the cauliflower is dry.

4 Tip the cauliflower into a large bowl. Add the eggs, cheese, salt, and pepper. Stir with a wooden spoon until well mixed.

5 Divide the mixture evenly between the baking sheets. Use the back of a spoon to spread the mixture out evenly and shape into an oval.

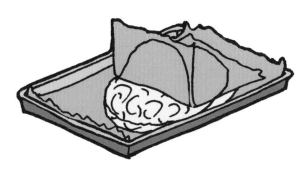

6 Bake for 30 minutes, or until firm. Wearing oven mitts and holding opposite corners of the paper, lift the bases off the sheets. Line the sheets with fresh paper. Flip the bases over and onto the sheets. Peel the paper off the top. Bake for 10 minutes.

7 Spread on the tomato paste, then top with the cheese, pepper, mushrooms, olives, and oregano. Bake for 15 minutes, or until the vegetables are cooked through and the cheese has melted. Slice and serve.

ZOODLES

Ingredients
4 large zucchini
1 tablespoon olive oil
your chosen sauce (see
    opposite page)

SERVES 4

TO SERVE
grated vegetarian Italian-
style hard cheese (optional)

1 Make your chosen sauce (see opposite page).

2 Trim the zucchini, then spiralize them, using the large noodle attachment on your spiralizer (see Tip).

3 Heat the oil in a large skillet over a medium heat.

4 Add the zoodles and fry for 2–3 minutes to soften.

5 Transfer to 4 plates and spoon over the sauce.

6 Sprinkle with grated cheese, if you like.

Tip

If you don't have a spiralizer, use a vegetable peeler to make long, thin strips of zucchini. Cut each strip into noodles with a sharp knife.

TOMATO SAUCE

Ingredients

1 tablespoon olive oil
1 garlic clove, minced
1 x 14-ounce can chopped
    tomatoes

handful of basil leaves,
    plus extra to serve
salt and pepper

1 Heat the oil in a large skillet over a low heat. Add the garlic and fry for 1 minute.

2 Tip in the tomatoes. Half-fill the can with water and add to the skillet. Stir in the basil. Bring to the boil, then turn down the heat and bubble gently. Cook for 20 minutes, stirring occasionally.

3 Season with salt and pepper and add a little more basil.

PESTO SAUCE

Ingredients

¼ cup pine nuts
¼ cup grated vegetarian
    Italian-style hard cheese

3 large handfuls of basil
¼ cup olive oil
1 garlic clove, peeled

1 Heat a small saucepan over a low heat. Add the pine nuts and toast gently until just starting to brown. (Keep an eye on them– they burn very quickly!)

2 Tip the pine nuts, cheese, basil, oil, and garlic into a food processor. Blitz until smooth.

RAINBOW SKEWERS

Ingredients

8 cherry tomatoes
1 orange bell pepper, diced
1 yellow bell pepper, diced
1 zucchini, sliced
1 eggplant, diced

FOR THE GLAZE
2 tablespoons olive oil
1 tablespoon honey
1 tablespoon balsamic
   vinegar

MAKES 8

Tip

If you're using wooden skewers, soak them in water for 30 minutes before you start. This will stop them from burning.

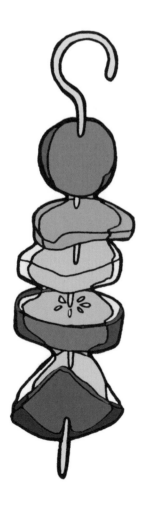

1 To make the glaze, put the oil, honey, and vinegar in a bowl and whisk together with a fork.

2 Thread the vegetables onto the skewers, following the colors of the rainbow. Be careful— skewers have very sharp ends.

3 Using a pastry brush, brush the vegetables with the glaze. Heat the broiler.

4 Put the skewers under the broiler for 10–12 minutes, turning every few minutes.

Variation

Fruit skewers make a delicious dessert. Try the following:

Ingredients

16 large white vegan
   marshmallows
8 small strawberries, stalks
   and hulls removed
8 mango chunks (fresh or
   frozen)
8 pineapple chunks (fresh or
   canned)
2 kiwi fruit, peeled and
   quartered
16 blueberries

MAKES 8

1 Thread a marshmallow
"cloud" onto each skewer.
Be careful–skewers have very
sharp ends.

2 Thread a strawberry onto
each skewer. Add the rest
of the fruit, following the
colors of the rainbow.

Tip

Drizzle the skewers with
your favorite chocolate
sauce before serving.

3 Finish each skewer with
a marshmallow. Heat the broiler.

4 Put the skewers under the
preheated broiler for 10 minutes,
turning every few minutes.

VEGGIE SAUSAGES & MASHED POTATOES

Ingredients

2 tablespoons olive oil, plus
   extra for brushing
½ onion, finely chopped
2 garlic cloves, minced
3 cups chopped chestnut
   mushrooms
sprig of thyme, leaves picked
1 x 14-ounce can cannellini
   beans, drained and rinsed
½ cup quick oats
1 tablespoon tomato paste
1 teaspoon smoked paprika
salt and pepper

SERVES 4

FOR THE MASHED POTATOES
4 large floury potatoes,
   peeled and cut into evenly
   sized chunks
2 tablespoons dairy-free
   spread
unsweetened coconut milk

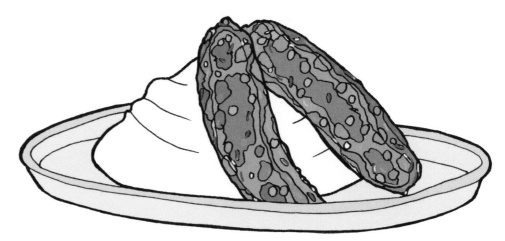

1 Heat 1 tablespoon of the oil in a large skillet over a low heat. Add the onion and fry for 10 minutes until soft. Add the garlic and cook for 1 minute. Tip into a large bowl and set aside.

2 Add the rest of the oil to the skillet. Turn the heat to high. Add the mushrooms and thyme. Cook for 5 minutes, stirring regularly. Tip into the bowl with the onion and garlic. Set aside to cool. (Don't wash up the skillet–you'll use it again later.)

3 To make the mashed potatoes, place a large saucepan of cold, salted water over a high heat. Bring to the boil, then add the potatoes. Cook for 15–20 minutes until tender.

4 Drain in a colander, then set over the saucepan to steam dry.

5 Tip the cooled mushroom mixture into a food processor. Add the beans, oats, tomato paste, paprika, and a little salt and pepper. Blend for a few seconds and then stop. Repeat until well mixed, but the mixture still has some texture (you don't want it to be too smooth).

6 Tip the sausage mixture back into the mixing bowl. Divide the mixture into 8 evenly-sized balls, then use your hands to shape into sausages.

7 Put the skillet over a medium heat. Brush the sausages all over with a little oil. Add to the skillet and fry for 5–10 minutes, turning occasionally, until golden brown all over (you might need to do this in batches).

8 Tip the potatoes back into the saucepan and mash with a potato masher until you can't see any lumps. Stir in the dairy-free spread, 1–2 splashes of milk, and a little salt and pepper. Mash until well mixed and smooth.

9 Spoon the mashed potatoes onto plates. Place the sausages on top and serve.

THAI GREEN CURRY

Ingredients

½ pound firm tofu, drained

1 tablespoon vegetable oil

bunch of scallions, trimmed, and sliced

small bunch of cilantro, leaves picked and stalks finely chopped

1 red bell pepper, seeded and sliced

handful of baby corn, halved lengthways

4 tablespoons Thai green curry paste

1 x 14-ounce can coconut milk

1 lime, zest and juice

handful of sugar snap peas

2 cups long-grain rice

TO SERVE

1 lime, cut into wedges

SERVES 4

1 Put the tofu between 2 clean dish towels and place a heavy saucepan on top (this will help to draw out the moisture). Set aside.

2 Meanwhile, heat the oil in a large skillet over a medium heat. Fry the scallions and cilantro stalks for 3 minutes, stirring regularly, until soft.

3 Add the bell pepper and corn to the skillet. Stir-fry for 5 minutes until starting to soften.

4 Stir in the curry paste. Cook for 2 minutes, stirring regularly.

5 Add the coconut milk, lime zest, and lime juice.

6 Cut the tofu into 1-inch cubes. Add to the skillet, along with the sugar snap peas. Bring to the boil, then turn the heat to low. Bubble gently for 10 minutes, or until the sugar snap peas are soft and the sauce has thickened.

7 While the curry is cooking, make the rice. Put the rice in a strainer and rinse it under the cold tap.

8 Tip the rice into a saucepan. Cover with cold water. Bring to the boil, then turn down the heat until bubbling gently. Put the lid on. Cook for 10 minutes, or until tender. Remove from the heat, drain off any remaining water, and set aside for a few minutes.

9 Add the cilantro leaves to the curry. Serve with the rice and lime wedges.

KATSU CURRY

Ingredients

vegetable oil, for greasing
1 cup all-purpose flour, sifted
1⅓ cups unsweetened soya milk
½ cup all-purpose flour
3 cups panko breadcrumbs, crushed
1 large cauliflower, cut into florets
salt and pepper

FOR THE CURRY SAUCE
1 tablespoon vegetable oil
2 teaspoons mild curry powder
1 teaspoon ground turmeric

SERVES 4-6

1 onion, finely sliced
2 garlic cloves, minced
1 x thumb-sized piece of root ginger, peeled and grated
1 x 14-ounce can coconut milk
2 tablespoons soy sauce

TO SERVE
1 x quantity cooked rice (see page 49)
½ carrot
¼ cucumber

1 Heat the oven to 425°F. Grease 2 large baking sheets.

2 Tip 1 cup flour into a large bowl and make a hole in the middle. Pour a little of the milk into the hole and whisk in a little flour from the sides. Continue, adding the milk a little at a time, until all the milk is used up and you have a smooth batter.

3 Put 2 wide, shallow bowls on the counter. Tip ½ cup flour into one and the breadcrumbs into the other. Season the flour with salt and pepper.

4 Dip a cauliflower floret into the flour, then into the batter, and then coat in breadcrumbs. Place on a baking sheet. Repeat with the rest of the cauliflower. Bake for 30–35 minutes, or until the cauliflower is tender and the coating is golden brown.

5 While the cauliflower nuggets are cooking, heat the oil in a large skillet over a medium heat. Add the curry powder and turmeric. Cook for 2 minutes, stirring regularly.

6 Turn the heat to low. Add the onion, garlic, and ginger. Cook for 10–15 minutes, or until soft.

7 Pour in the coconut milk. Bubble gently for 15 minutes, then stir in the soy sauce. While the sauce is cooking, make the rice (see page 49).

8 Use a vegetable peeler to make long ribbons of carrot and cucumber.

9 Place a large spoonful of rice onto each plate. Top with curry sauce, cauliflower nuggets, and vegetable ribbons.

MIXED BEAN CHILI

Ingredients

2 tablespoons olive oil
1 red onion, finely chopped
2 garlic cloves, minced
1/2 tablespoon ground paprika
1/2 tablespoon ground cumin
2 teaspoon mild chili powder
2 x 14-ounce cans chopped tomatoes
pinch of sugar
1 x 14-ounce can kidney beans,
     drained and rinsed
1 x 14-ounce can black beans,
     drained and rinsed

TO SERVE
1 x quantity cooked rice (see page 49)
grated vegetarian Cheddar cheese

SERVES 4

1 Heat the oil in a large skillet over a low heat. Fry the onion for 5–10 minutes until soft.

2 Stir in the garlic, paprika, cumin, and chili powder. Cook for 1 minute.

3 Add the tomatoes and sugar. Turn up the heat, bring to the boil, then turn the heat to low. Put a lid on the skillet and bubble gently for 20 minutes. While the chili is cooking, make the rice (see page 49).

4 Stir the beans into the chili. Cook without a lid for 5 minutes.

5 Divide the rice between 4 plates or bowls. Spoon over the chili and sprinkle with a little grated cheese.

Variation

Try serving the chili with baked potatoes, quinoa, couscous, or fresh bread, or inside a burrito or taco.

EXTRA TOPPING IDEAS
* sliced avocado * Guacamole (see page 9)
* tortilla chips * salsa * vegetarian
sour cream * lime wedges

BLUEBERRY PANCAKES

Ingredients

1½ cups self-rising flour
1 teaspoon baking powder
1 egg
1 cup milk

1 tablespoon unsalted butter, melted, plus extra for frying
1 cup blueberries

MAKES 8-10

1 Sift the flour and baking powder into a large bowl. Using a wooden spoon, make a large hole in the middle of the flour.

2 Crack the egg into a pitcher. Add the milk. Beat together with a fork until smooth.

3 Pour a little egg mixture into the middle of the flour. Bring some flour into the middle. Whisk until smooth. Continue until the egg mixture is used up and you have a smooth batter.

4 Stir in the melted butter and blueberries.

5 Heat a little butter in a large skillet over a medium heat. Drop in spoonfuls of batter, leaving space between each one (you'll need to cook 3 or 4 at a time).

6 Cook for 2–3 minutes, or until small bubbles appear on the surface of each pancake.

7 Flip over with a spatula. Cook for 2 minutes until golden and firm. Serve with maple or golden syrup.

BANANA PANCAKES

Ingredients

2 very ripe bananas
2 eggs
1 cup self-rising flour
vegetable oil, for frying

MAKES 8-10

Variation

For vegan pancakes, replace the eggs with
2 tablespoons dairy-free milk.

1 In a large bowl, mash the bananas with a fork until smooth.

2 Whisk in the eggs.

3 Sift in the flour. Whisk until well mixed.

4 Heat a little oil in a large skillet over a medium heat. Drop in tablespoonfuls of batter, leaving space between each one (you'll need to cook 3 or 4 at a time).

5 Cook for 2–3 minutes, or until small bubbles appear on the surface of each pancake.

6 Flip over with a spatula. Cook for 2 minutes until golden and firm. Serve with maple or golden syrup.

ZUCCHINI BROWNIES

Adding grated zucchini to chocolate brownies makes them super fudgy and moist. They'll keep for up to 4 days in an airtight container, or you can freeze them for up to a month.

Ingredients
$^2/_3$ cup vegetable oil, plus extra for greasing
$1^1/_2$ cups superfine sugar
2 cups all-purpose flour
$^1/_2$ cup cocoa powder
$1^1/_2$ teaspoons baking soda
pinch of salt
$1^1/_2$ cups grated zucchini

MAKES 12

1 Heat the oven to 350°F. Grease an 8 x 12-inch baking pan and line it with parchment paper.

2 In a large bowl, whisk together the oil and sugar.

3 Sift in the flour, cocoa powder, baking soda, and salt. Fold in with a large metal spoon until well mixed.

4 Gently fold in the zucchini.

5 Spoon into the pan and smooth the top. Bake for 25–30 minutes until just firm in the center.

6 Leave to cool in the pan before cutting into squares.

Variation

Zucchini isn't the only vegetable you can add to brownies. You could try grated carrot or parsnip.

BUTTERNUT SQUASH COOKIES

Ingredients

1 cup dairy-free spread
1 cup superfine sugar
1 cup dark brown sugar
½ butternut squash, roasted and cooled (see Tip, page 23)
3 cups all-purpose flour, sifted, plus extra for dusting
1 cup quick oats
1 teaspoon baking powder
¾ teaspoon baking soda
1 teaspoon salt
1 teaspoon mixed spice (optional)

FOR THE FROSTING
1 cup confectioners' sugar, sifted
5 teaspoons lemon juice

MAKES 24

1 Beat together the spread, superfine sugar, and brown sugar in a large bowl, using a wooden spoon or an electric whisk, until pale and fluffy.

2 Scoop out the butternut squash flesh and put ¾ cup into a bowl. Mash with a fork until smooth.

3 Stir the mashed squash into the butter and sugar mixture.

4 Fold in the flour, oats, baking powder, baking soda, salt, and mixed spice (if using).

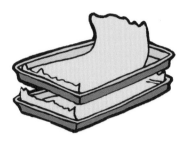

5 Bring the dough together into a ball. Cover in plastic wrap and put in the refrigerator for 1 hour.

6 Heat the oven to 400°F. Line 2 large baking sheets with parchment paper.

7 Lightly dust your hands and the counter with flour. Roll the dough into 24 evenly sized balls (about the size of a golf ball). Put on the baking sheets, leaving space between each one.

8 Bake for 15 minutes. Allow to cool on the trays for a few minutes, then transfer to a wire rack to cool.

9 Once cool, make the frosting. Put the icing sugar in a small bowl. Stir in the lemon juice a little at a time until the frosting is smooth and glossy.

10 Drizzle or pipe the frosting on in a zigzag pattern.

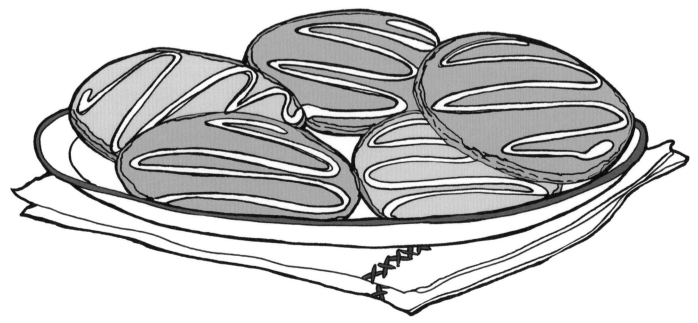

CHOCOLATE & BEET CAKE

Ingredients

1 cup vegetable oil, plus extra
   for greasing
1/2 pound cooked beet (in
   natural juices, not
   vinegar), chopped
2 eggs
1 1/2 cups all-purpose flour
3/4 cup cocoa powder
2 teaspoons baking powder
1 1/4 cups superfine sugar

FOR THE FROSTING
1/4 cup (1/2 stick) unsalted
   butter, softened
1 1/2 cups confectioners' sugar,
   sifted
1/2 cup full-fat cream cheese

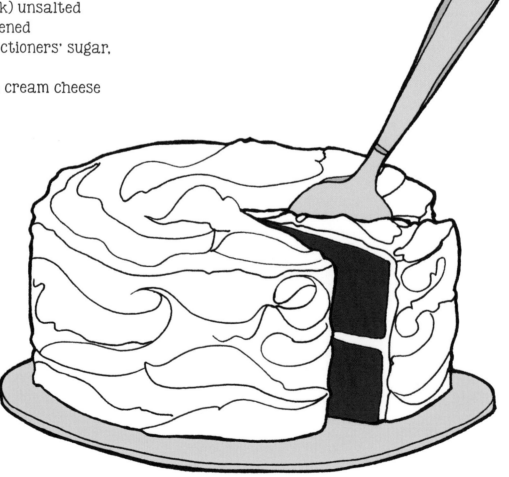

1 Heat the oven to 400°F. Grease 2 x 20cm cake pans. Line the bases with parchment paper.

2 Put the oil, beet, and eggs in a food processor. Blend until smooth. Tip into a large bowl.

3 Sift in the flour, cocoa powder, and baking powder. Tip in the superfine sugar. Fold in with a large metal spoon until well mixed. Divide equally between the pans.

4 Bake for 20–25 minutes, or until a skewer inserted into the center comes out clean. Allow to cool in the pans, then turn out onto a wire rack.

5 To make the frosting, put the butter in a bowl. Beat in the confectioners' sugar a little at a time, using a wooden spoon or electric whisk, until smooth.

6 Beat in half the cream cheese. Add the rest and beat until smooth.

Tip

To decorate the cake, dust with 1-2 tablespoons sifted cocoa powder or grate over a little bittersweet chocolate.

7 Once the cakes are completely cool, spread some frosting onto one cake. Place the other cake on top. Spread the rest of the frosting over the top and sides.

FRUIT & ROOT ROLL-UPS

Fruit roll-ups (sometimes called fruit leathers) are easy to prepare, but they do need a long time in the oven. It can take up to 5 hours for them to dry out, so why not get creative with some fruit and vegetables while you wait? (See Tip.)

Ingredients

4 cups frozen strawberries
1¼ cups chopped carrot
2 Braeburn or Gala apples,
    cored and cut into chunks

MAKES 10-12

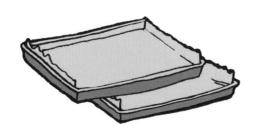

1 Line 2 baking sheets with parchment paper.

2 Put the strawberries, carrot, and apple in a large saucepan. Put over a low heat. Cover with a lid. Cook for 30 minutes, or until the carrot and apple are soft.

3 Remove from the heat and allow to cool a little. Tip into a food processor. Blend to a smooth purée.

4 Using a wooden spoon, push the purée through a strainer into a clean saucepan.

5 Put the saucepan over a medium heat. Cook, stirring occasionally, for about 10 minutes, or until thickened. When it's ready, you should be able to pull the spoon through the purée and see the bottom of the saucepan.

6 Heat the oven to its lowest setting. Divide the mixture between the sheets, spreading the purée out thinly and evenly. Bake for 3–5 hours, or until it's no longer sticky, but is still bendy.

7 Cut into strips using a pizza cutter or scissors (make sure you cut through the paper too).

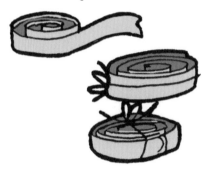

8 Roll up and tie with string. Store in an airtight container.

Tip

While you wait, have a go at creating some colorful prints with fruit and vegetables. You could use trimmings for this, such as the base of a bell pepper or a broccoli stem, or fruits that are past their best. Just cut them up to create interesting shapes, dip them in paint, and print onto paper. The bottom half of a baby gem lettuce makes a lovely rose, and you can use orange halves to create a striking tie-dye effect.

First published 2022 by Button Books, an imprint of Guild of Master Craftsman Publications Ltd. Text © GMC Publications Ltd, 2022. Copyright in the Work © GMC Publications Ltd, 2022. Illustrations © Esther Coombs, 2022. Recipes by Laura Paton. ISBN 978 1 78708 119 2. Distributed by Publishers Group West in the United States. All rights reserved. The right of Esther Coombs to be identified as the illustrator of this work has been asserted in accordance with the Copyright, Designs, and Patents Act 1988, sections 77 and 78. No part of this publication may be reproduced, stored in a retrieval system, or transmitted in any form or by any means without the prior permission of the publisher and copyright owner. This book is sold subject to the condition that all designs are copyright and are not for commercial reproduction without the permission of the designer and copyright owner. The publishers and author can accept no legal responsibility for any consequences arising from the application of information, advice, or instructions given in this publication. Printed and bound in China.

FSC
MIX
Paper
FSC® C020056